A Gift For

_____

From

_____

100 Bible Verses
to Bless Your
Baby Boy

Editor: Lindsay Evans
Art Director: Kevin Swanson
Designer: Craig Bissell
Production Designer: Bryan Ring

ISBN: 978-1-59530-380-6
BOK1166

Printed and bound in China
JAN15

100 Bible Verses to Bless Your Baby Boy

By Jack Countryman

Hallmark
gift books

Introduction

*God has chosen you to be one of His children
and has created you to be a reflection of
His love. The Bible is God's pathway to life,
and the verses contained in this book were
written as encouragement to you. May you
be drawn closer to God as you hear what
He has written just for you. The topics that
have been chosen will enrich your life and bring
you to a more meaningful relationship with our
Heavenly Father. As you experience these verses
of Scripture, may the guidance and joy of
God's Word bring peace and contentment
to your heart.*

Contents

You Were Created by God

Before I made you in your mother's womb,
I chose you.

Jeremiah 1:5

The work of God in a mother's womb is truly
a wonder to behold. You were woven together
in a unique and different way, unlike anyone else.
Each life has been established from the beginning
by God for a special purpose.

The Holy Spirit will guide you, protect you,
and surround you with His everlasting love.

A Lesson Every Child
Must Learn

Trust the Lord, you will be safe.
Proverbs 29:25

Trust, in the Bible, is mentioned over fifty times.
This is one of God's greatest desires for you.
He wants you to trust Him in everything you
may do. Growing up is a challenge, but when you
learn to trust in the Lord, you will find rest.
He is ready and waiting just for you.

Trust in the Lord is the beginning of
God-given wisdom.

3

God Loves a Thankful Heart

It is good to praise you, Lord,
to sing praises to God Most High.

Psalm 92:1

When you sing and give praises to God
for the marvelous gifts He has given you,
there is a certain joy that will fill your heart.
You will be filled with the contentment only
He can give. Sing often and give thanks to the
One who has blessed you with a beautiful life.

Thank God each day for giving
you the joy of your life.

God's Protection

I am with you and will protect you
everywhere you go.

Genesis 28:15

One of the beautiful promises God has given
you is that He will always be with you to guide
your steps and protect you. God will always stay
with you and keep His promise, even when you
go through the storms of life. When life causes
you to wonder if He is really there,
you can rest assured He is.

There is someone who is closer than you can
imagine. Rest in His presence.

5

Trust in an Absolute

Trust the Lord with all your heart.
Proverbs 3:5

One of the great essentials in life is to learn what
it means to trust in the Lord with all your heart.
The foundation that is established early in life
will help you develop a strong sense of moral
character in knowing what is right and what is
wrong. God's guidance is more than sufficient
for all the tests and trials you may have to face.
You will soon discover tests come in all shapes
and sizes. God wants you to come to Him
for all the wisdom you need.

Dependence on God is much like leaning on
a giant oak tree. It will never fall down!

6

The God of Our Salvation

Our God is a God who saves us.
Psalm 68:20

When you were given the beautiful gift of life,
you were granted the privilege to discover
how much God, through His tender mercy,
loves and cares for you each day that you allow
Him to do so. God is on your side. Invite Him
in to every area of your life.

"Bless the Lord, who daily loads us with benefits."

God Has Promised
to Always Be with You

I will make you strong and will help you.
I will support you with my right hand
that saves you.

Isaiah 41:10b

God's Word is strong and true. He has promised
to be with you in all circumstances. What you
do with that promise is what matters most.
You are God's child, therefore never be afraid.
You have the power to overcome fear, for when
you apply His Word to your life, He will
protect and sustain you.

What God has given, no one can take away.

8

Jesus Welcomes You

Let the little children come to me.
Don't stop them, because the kingdom
of heaven belongs to people who are
like these children.

Matthew 19:14

You can always count on Jesus. He wants
very much for you to enjoy the love and care
of our Heavenly Father. Through your life, the
stories you read and the songs you sing will bring
you joy and contentment. You will never be too
old to learn about the love of God.

God is very passionate about your welfare.

God Will Take Care of You

He takes care of his people like a shepherd.
He gathers them like lambs in his arms
and carries them close to him. He gently leads
the mothers of the lambs.

Isaiah 40:11

God has promised to take care of you always—
especially when you look to Him for guidance.
He will carry you close to Him, and His care is
gentle and full of love. Daily seek God's guidance
for wisdom to grow and mature in His love.

Jesus is both God's Lamb and our Shepherd.

10

You Are One of a Kind by God's Design

The Lord is good to everyone;
he is merciful to all he has made.

Psalm 145:9

There is never a doubt that you are special
in God's eyes. His creation is one of a kind, and
you have been blessed with the privilege of the
life He gave you. God's merciful character has
showered you with a beautiful blessing.
What God has created bears the mark of
His wonder. Therefore, be happy and rejoice
with the gift you have been given.

God is the Great Provider. He gives to all life,
breath, and all things.

11

God Is Watching Over You

*When you lie down, you won't be afraid . . .
because the Lord will keep you safe.*

Proverbs 3:24a, 26a

There will be times in your life when you will be
upset and feel as though nothing is going your
way. Rest assured that God has placed within
you the ability to handle any situation that might
come your way. When you pray, He will give you
guidance so that you might be sensitive to
His leading and gain His wisdom.

*"Little ones to Him belong.
They are weak but He is strong."*

You Were Made in His Image

You made my whole being;
you formed me in my mother's body.

Psalm 139:13

The work of God in your life extends back
to your development in the womb. God's
creation is an awesome wonder, and each one
is "fearfully and wonderfully made." When you
came into the world, innocence, purity,
and the very air of heaven came along to live,
grow, and develop into the child that was
created in God's image.

God's compassion is extended to every life
He has created.

Nothing Ever Escapes
God's View

*You saw my bones being formed as
I took shape in my mother's body.*
Psalm 139:15

Your life and structure were all established from
the beginning by God. The formation of each toe,
finger, and entire body was under God's care and
formed just as He intended. That is why
you are so very special. God loves you just
as you are—the way He made you.
You belong to Him—lock, stock,
and barrel—without question.

*We are children of God, and our Father
eagerly seeks to speak to us.*

14

God Wants You to Be Faithful

Parents who have wise children
are glad because of them.
Proverbs 23:24b

God has designed you to be the person
He wishes for you to be. He has placed within
your heart a certain love that only He can give.
From the very moment you came into the
world, He was faithfully providing the building
blocks for your character. As you grow,
each day will be filled with His presence.
You are precious in His sight.

The lessons you learn today
will bring great rewards tomorrow.

15

You Can Count on God

I will never leave you nor forsake you.
Hebrews 13:5b (NKJV)

This is one of the great promises from the Bible.
You have a true companion that cares more
about you than you can imagine. When God is
included in all that you do, you and your entire
family will be blessed. Jesus loves you. Night,
morning, and every day. He hears and answers
your prayers. He is always beside you whether
in work or when you play.

*Christ's grace is presently and permanently
available to all who believe in Him.*

16

God's Love Never Changes

Lord, you do everything for me.
Lord, your love continues forever.

Psalm 138:8

God loves you with an everlasting love that
will never change. Bask daily in His love,
share His precious Word, and pray daily for
His divine guidance. God will come to you when
you humbly seek Him, because He has promised
to be with you always. His Spirit will help you.

God's gifts put your best dreams to shame.

17

You Are Under God's Protection

I will cover you with my hands and protect you.
Isaiah 51:16b

Fear and worry are never necessary when
you walk beside our Heavenly Father.
He has promised to cover you, to protect you
from harm. He will not leave you comfortless,
and He will always come to you with words
of hope and mercy. When you are hurt,
His goal is not to break you, but to teach you
and draw you close to Him in times of
heartache and extreme pressure.

The Word of God is like a sharp sword.
Use it for your protection.

You Are God's Gift

Be careful. Don't think these little children are worth nothing. I tell you that they have angels in heaven who are always with my Father in heaven.

Matthew 18:10

In the eyes of God, you are precious. His love for you is unconditional and everlasting. Every gift God has given you is worth celebrating. You are blessed, and He is watching over you. Let the joy of the Lord fill your heart with love and laughter.

God is watching over you.

19

We Are God's Reflection, We Belong to Him

Know that the Lord is God.
He made us, and we belong to him;
we are his people, the sheep he tends.

Psalm 100:3

God is the Shepherd, and we are His flock.
God is the Creator, we are His creation.
God is the Father, we are His children.
When you remember this basic truth,
your spirit will be filled with His unending
love for you. Let each day be filled with
His presence, and you will be blessed.

The more we invite the Lord into our lives,
His loving, holy nature grows.

Wisdom and Understanding
Are God-Given

*It takes wisdom to have a good family,
and it takes understanding to make it strong.*

Proverbs 24:3

Everyone is talented and gifted in some way.
Seek early the wisdom and understanding
that only God can provide. When you come
to the Lord with an open heart, He will provide
you with everything you will need and desire.
You are precious in God's eyes;
seek His direction, and you will be blessed.

*The supreme happiness in life is the
evidence we are loved.*

God's Design Is Perfect

He will show compassion according to the
multitude of His mercies. He does not afflict
willingly, nor grieve the children of men.
Lamentations 3:32b-33 (NKJV)

When you belong to God, you can face life with
great confidence. God's compassion and mercy
are all that you need. God's unchanging nature
teaches you that even when you feel unlovely,
you remain beautiful to Him. You can do nothing
to change His love for you—it's unconditional
and flows freely from the throne of grace.

All is well if it is in God's hands.

22

Children Are Precious to God

*Whoever accepts a child in
my name accepts me.*
Matthew 18:5

You are important to God. He has created you
in His image and wants the very best for you.
God has a special purpose just for you and wants
you to grow and live so that His name will be
honored. He knows everything about you and
wants for you to be a blessing to others.

To God, you are always important.

23

Jesus Is the Giver of Life

I have come that they may have life,
and that they may have it more abundantly.
John 10:10b (NKJV)

God's greatest desire is for you to have
a life filled with joy, peace, happiness, and
the contentment only He can provide.
If Jesus willingly gave His life to save you,
He would never hold back anything that
would benefit you. He is the Good Shepherd
who gives life to His sheep.

When Jesus makes an offer,
no one can take it away.

God's Commitment Is Everlasting

I have loved you with an everlasting love.
Jeremiah 31:3b (NKJV)

God's love is so wonderful because it is
everlasting. From the very first moment you
were conceived, you were loved. When your
mother carried you in her womb, you were loved.
When birth was given and you entered into the
world, you were loved. As you grew and began to
talk, you were loved. God has pledged His love
to you. He walks with you in every circumstance.
He has finished your portrait. Through Christ,
you can and will be successful.

God's love is unconditional.

God Protects Those Who Know Him

He has put his angels in charge of you
to watch over you wherever you go.
They will catch you in their hands.

Psalm 91:11–12

God provides His angels to watch over you.
When you ask for His protection, He will be
there. God wants your relationship with Him
to be filled with joy and gladness. You are
His advertisement to the world of His goodness
and mercy. You have been promised God's
protection; therefore, do not hesitate to seek
God's wisdom, and pray daily to help you with
the responsibilities you have been given.

You are always protected by God.

God Has Broad Shoulders

*I have leaned on you since the day
I was born; you have been my God
since my mother gave me birth.*

Psalm 22:10

God desires that you trust in Him with all your heart. He will watch over you in whatever you do. He belongs to you and wants you to belong to Him. When you lean on Him daily and learn to come to Him with all your needs, wants, and cares, He will always be there for you.

You can trust God.

27

With the Lord,
Fear Is Unnecessary

The Lord is my light and the one who saves me.
Psalm 27:1

God says you need not be afraid of the dark
when the Lord gives you light. He provides
comfort when you are afraid. You need not fear
anything when you walk in the power of
God's Spirit. Ask Him to help you be the light
that brings peace and comfort to everyone you
know. When God is your guide, you will find all
the peace and confidence you will ever need.

Perfect love casts out fear.
1 John 4:18 NKJV

28

Jesus Paid the
Ultimate Price for You

*God loved the world so much that he gave
his one and only Son so that whoever believes
in him may not be lost, but have eternal life.*

John 3:16

God loves you so much that He was willing
to give His one and only Son that you might have
life everlasting. He has that same love for you
and wants your life to be filled with joy and
happiness. His love for you is like a circle that
had a beginning when you arrived and has no
ending. It keeps going around, ever expanding
and growing as you become the person
God wants you to be.

The love of Christ is within you.

29

God's Indescribable Gift

Thanks be to God for His indescribable gift.
2 Corinthians 9:15 (NKJV)

You have been given a gift that will not be
given to anyone else. You are special, a treasure
that is unique and cannot be duplicated.
You have been given a purpose in life that will
fill you with pleasure. Speak loving words of
comfort, sing sweet songs of joy. Thank God
for His marvelous gift of grace.

God's greatest gift is Jesus.

You Are a Miracle in God's Eyes

Every perfect gift is from God.
These good gifts come down from the
Creator of the sun, moon, and stars.

James 1:17

When you came into the world, a miracle was created by God. The gift of life was given to you. As you grow and experience life, you will have moments of laughter, tears, sickness, and good health. Each one of these is a steppingstone to becoming the person God has designed you to be.

Miracles happen and you are one of them.

Help Is Just a Prayer Away

My help comes from the Lord.
Psalm 121:2

God never intended for you to go through life
alone. As you need guidance, you can turn to
Him for help. His peace will surround you
in times of chaos and joy in each new experience
you encounter. Therefore, invite God to be
your helper, and let Him embrace you
and be your blessing-giver.

God's wisdom is there for the asking.

God Has a Plan for You

God is working in you to help you want to do
and be able to do what pleases him.
Philippians 2:13

God has always had a plan for your life.
You are one of a kind by God's design.
Everything about you is special; you are
cherished, loved, and enjoyed as you develop
into everything God wants you to be.
May you grow up with a thankful heart and
be a blessing and a shining light to the world.

God loves you because you are His child.

You Are a Blessing

*I will cause showers to come down in their
season; there shall be showers of blessing.*

Ezekiel 34:26 (NKJV)

You are a blessing to those who love you.
The precious moments of your childhood will
seem to fade and become memories as you grow
older. Enjoy every moment God has given you.

*Your early years are to be remembered,
recorded, and enjoyed.*

34

Grace and Mercy
Are God's Gifts

The Lord has mercy on those who respect him,
as a father has mercy on his children.

Psalm 103: 13

God wants every part of you—body, soul,
and spirit—to grow close to Him and enter into a
joyful relationship with Him. He openly wants to
bless you when you choose to please Him
first in your life and gladly give everything
you are to Him.

God cares for you as a good father
cares for His children.

Children Are a Heritage

Children are a gift from the Lord;
babies are a reward.

Psalm 127:3

You are a bundle of blessings. As you grow older,
you will be a comfort and joy to others. You can
be a positive influence to the next generation.
The virtues and qualities God has given you
will become an important model of the person
God wishes you to be. His love will guide you
and go before you as you learn to trust Him
in all that you do.

A positive role model will make a
lasting impression.

Trusting God Is Looking Beyond What We Can Do

When I am afraid, I will trust you.

Psalm 56:3

Learning to trust God is a lifelong process.
As a baby naturally trusts its mother,
learn to trust God early. Fear is a natural human
reaction to danger. God does not tell us to
ignore our fears but bring them to Him.
When we say "I will trust," these are words
of confidence even in times of distress.
Therefore, build each day a sense of trust in God.

*Trusting God means looking beyond
what we can see to what God sees.*

Learn From Your Parents

My son, keep your father's commands,
and don't forget your mother's teaching.
Keep their words in mind forever.
They will guide you when you walk.

Proverbs 6:20–21a, 22a

As you grow and understand right from wrong,
the teachings of your parents will become clearer.
God wants you to listen carefully to your parents
and learn from their wisdom.

God's way leads to life.

God Is the Great Provider

The Lord is my shepherd;
I have everything I need.

Psalm 23:1

If you have the Lord, you have everything.
He will always meet your needs. May you know
the Lord as your Shepherd and Savior. Grow to
love God, and He will bless you. Learn to trust
Him with all your heart, and He will protect you.
Look to Him for wisdom and understanding,
and success will find you.

The Good Shepherd will pardon,
provide, and protect you.

39

You Are an Awesome Wonder

*I praise you because you made me
in an amazing and wonderful way.
What you have done is wonderful.*

Psalm 139:14

Praise God for His marvelous creation.
You are one of a kind, conceived and woven
together. You are the work of God—a truly
awesome wonder. Every part of you is a skillful
demonstration of the creative power of God,
who has a special plan and purpose for your life.

You are God's precious creation.

40

The Lord Is Faithful

The Lord will keep all his promises;
he is loyal to all he has made.

Psalm 145:13b

All that God has made bears the marks of
His hand. You are a part of His marvelous
creation. You can count on His mercy and love
in all that you do. With each step you take
and each word you speak, He will be with you.
Learn early in your life the message of His grace
and forgiveness. He is the One who loves you
with an everlasting love.

Everything the Lord does is right.

God Hears Your Prayers

The Lord is close to everyone
who prays to him.
Psalm 145:18

Prayers that you learn early in life are like
seeds planted in the ground. Every time you pray,
spiritual water helps you grow and develop into
the person God intends you to be. Let the daily
habit of coming to God in prayer be one of the
first things you learn. You will be blessed, and
your Heavenly Father will be glorified.

God is patiently waiting to hear your prayer.

Love Produces a Bond That Cannot Be Broken

The Lord protects everyone who loves him.

Psalm 145:20

Our Heavenly Father knows everything about us and has an abundant love for us just the way we are. He knows how we are made, He knows our weaknesses, He knows our strengths, He knows our every desire and our innermost hurts, fears, and frustrations, and yet He longs to have a loving intimate relationship with us.

We belong to God.

God Is Our Sure Defense

God is our refuge and strength,
a very present help in trouble.

Psalm 46:1 (NKJV)

There will be times when you are sick
or so upset that you may feel that your world
has been shaken, you are at your wits' end,
where everything you depend upon seems
to be falling apart. If you are patient and put
your hope in God, you have no need to fear
or be frustrated, because you have a refuge
in Him that can never be moved.

Be calm, be patient, this, too, will pass.

Obedience to Christ Pays Dividends

God gives us what we ask for because we obey God's commands and do what pleases him.

1 John 3:22

As a parent wishes his child to be obedient to what he asks, so God wishes the same for you. When you do what is right, pure, and honorable, the Lord will bless you, protect you, and guide your every step. God takes everything you do into account. He is more compassionate and understanding toward you than you are toward yourself.

When we are one with God,
everything becomes right.

Your Life Should Be Filled with Love

God is love. Those who live in love live in God, and God lives in them. This is how love is made perfect in us.

1 John 4:16–17a

You were born with the love of God within your heart. When you live in the love of God, you will naturally live and grow in that same model. When you emulate God's love, those around you respond to your care and thoughtfulness. When God's love is perfected in you, the confidence you have in Christ and your Christian walk will naturally flow to others.

There is nothing more important than the love you share with others.

46

Pure Thoughts Are a Blessing

*They are blessed whose thoughts
are pure, for they will see God.*

Matthew 5:8

Today's culture creates many challenges for
people to have pure thoughts. Television,
the Internet, movies, and the acceptable worldly
lifestyle have created obstacles for everyone to
combat as they strive for the pure thoughts God
so desires for His children. Read God's Word
daily to build the foundation of good thoughts
that will create a blessing.

*Your faith causes others to wonder
what they're missing.*

Nothing Can Separate You from the Love of God

*Nothing above us, nothing below us,
nor anything else in the whole world will ever
be able to separate us from the love of God
that is in Christ Jesus our Lord.*

Romans 8:39

You have been created in God's image, and
from the beginning, He has set His love on you.
When we accept His love through faith in Jesus,
nothing can ever break the bonds of love that
He creates and "no one is able to snatch them out
of our Father's hands." If God the uncreated
One is for us, then nothing can separate us
from the One who created us.

Our security in Him is absolute.

Learn Respect Early

*Honor your father and your mother so that
you will live a long time in the land.*

Exodus 20:12

When honor and respect are part of your family
process, you will soon learn what is acceptable
and what is not. With every commandment
from the Bible, there was a blessing for
obedience. He gave you those commandments
to prepare you for life. There are certain habits
that will develop honor and a strong moral
character that only He can give. Learn early
what is acceptable in God's eyes,
and you will be blessed.

Honoring God is the highest priority in your life.

49

Following the Rules Is the Beginning of Wisdom

Your rules are wonderful. That is why I keep them. Learning your words gives wisdom.
Psalm 119:129-130

God's desire for every child is that he will learn
the rules of life early and profit from each lesson.
Wisdom is a gift that is given when anyone is
willing to listen. Strive to become a good listener,
and follow the rules. When you are successful,
you will grow to know what is acceptable
and you will be blessed with the discernment
to understand right from wrong.

Wisdom is a precious treasure; learn it early in life.

Everything Belongs to God

The earth belongs to the Lord, and everything
in it—the world and all its people.

Psalm 24:1

You belong to God, and everything that is
made or ever will be made belongs to Him.
He is sovereign over all He has created.
You have been created to honor Him and be
a blessing to those who love you and care for
you. He wants you to know that He loves you
and will love you forever with an affection
that nothing and no one can take away.
You are God's special gift.

He saves us for His namesake and for His glory.

Believers Are Blessed

*Everyone who believes that Jesus
is the Christ is God's child.*

1 John 5:1a

You have been created to be a blessing to those
who love you. Each day, you will learn and grow
into your own special personality. In time,
you will learn that love for God is not merely
a warm sentiment or a pleasant feeling; it is a
living, active force that changes who you are.

Let God's love shine brightly in all you become.

You Are Special

Before I made you in your mother's womb,
I chose you.

Jeremiah 1:5a

You are not an accident, nor did you come along
by chance. Before you took your first breath,
God knew everything about you. He even knew
your name. He is by your side, and you are living
in His presence. In each step you take and
every word you speak, God is with you and
is personally, intimately abiding in you.
You are very special to Him.

The Lord is your Helper.

53

God Will Take Care of You

*I sing to the Lord because
he has taken care of me.*

Psalm 13:6

God loves you and promised to be with you
from the very moment you were born.
Everything about you is special to God, and
He wants you to grow and become someone
who will reflect who He is and bring Him glory.
Since the Lord is righteous, He wants you to
grow and act in a righteous way. Through His
Spirit, He will give you exactly what you need.

God is ever by your side.

God Is Your Best Cheerleader

*May he give you what you want and
make all your plans succeed, and we will shout
for joy when you succeed.*

Psalm 20:4–5a

God has one great desire for you and that is for
you to succeed in everything you choose to do.
You have been created for a special purpose.
He will love you with a love that outlasts all
human love. He has promised a love that will
endure every test and be loyal to you through
a lifetime of success and failure.

You can count on God in every way.

55

God Gives Us
All Things to Enjoy

God wants all people to eat and drink and be happy in their work, which are gifts from God.
Ecclesiastes 3:13

God desires that your life be filled with joy and happiness. From the moment you are born, His love surrounds you. Whatever talents you may have are gifts from God; therefore, let His light shine through you. Learn early to trust in Him for all things, and give Him your very best effort in all that you do.

True joy comes from the Living God.

56

Learn About God Early

Remember your Creator while you are young.

Ecclesiastes 12:1

Never forget who has created you and the
purpose He has for your life. Let each day be
filled with words of love, joy, and peace from
the Bible. Sing "Jesus loves me, this I know, for
the Bible tells me so, little ones to Him belong,
they are weak but He is strong. Yes, Jesus loves
me, yes, Jesus loves me, yes, Jesus loves me,
the Bible tells me so." Plant these words in
your heart, and they will be there forever.

The thoughts that are planted early
will last for a lifetime.

Giving Is a Way of Life

I taught you to remember the words Jesus said:
"It is more blessed to give than to receive."
Acts 20:35b

There is a natural instinct to selfishly look
out for yourself. The words me and mine are
naturally a part of everyone's vocabulary.
God's way is different. When you give of
your time, talent, finances, and possessions,
true happiness finds you. When others are
more important than yourself, life becomes
meaningful. Paul, in the Bible, found his life by
losing it. He lived his life by not counting it dear.
When he learned to love God's will over
everything else, he realized that obeying
God yielded the greatest joy of life.

Giving to others is living out the love of God.

God's Gift for Everyone

God gives us the free gift of life forever
in Christ Jesus our Lord.

Romans 6:23b

From the moment you are born, God,
through His love and tender mercy,
offers the gift of eternal life. As you grow,
you can fully enjoy God's blessings by learning
to live by faith. He wraps you in His loving care,
and His love toward you never changes.
Every good thing that happens in your life
is by His grace that will wash over you like
sunlight on a cloudless day.

God loves you just the way you are.

You Are Precious

You are precious to me, because
I give you honor and love you.

Isaiah 43:4a

Because God created you in His image,
you are precious to Him. Because God created
you for His glory, He wants the world to see
some of His majesty and goodness through you,
and He wants to crown you with His own
splendor. He has not promised to keep you out
of the wilderness or away from the desert, but if
you belong to Him, He does promise to sustain
you and renew your life when times are difficult.

You can always count on God.

60

You Are God's Masterpiece

The Lord your God is with you;
the mighty one will save you. He will rejoice
over you. You will rest in his love; he will
sing and be joyful about you.

Zephaniah 3:17

God rejoices over you, and He knows you are
in the process of becoming all that He has
planned for you to become. You are not yet
what you will be, but He is patiently molding and
shaping you into His image. He is always with
you, cheering you on, and encouraging you along
the way. Fix your eyes on Him, and you will
begin to see life differently. The more you grow,
the Holy Spirit will teach you to think about
the things of God.

God has promised over and over to love you.

61

Trust and Hope
Go Hand in Hand

*We rejoice in him, because we trust his
holy name. Lord, show your love to us
as we put our hope in you.*

Psalm 33:21–22

When you learn to trust in God with all
your heart, everything in life falls into place.
You soon recognize that God is the One in
charge and He is full of hope. When dependence
on Him becomes your way of life, things that
seem difficult disappear. By His mercy, He knows
what you need and wants you to be happy in all
that you do. God stands ready to help you make
the right choices. Look to Him daily to
experience a deep fellowship with Him.

Put your hope and trust in God.

Eternal Life Is a
Gift from God

*God has given us eternal life, and this life is
in his Son. Whoever has the Son has life.*

1 John 5:11–12a

God has promised you eternal life through
His Son, Jesus Christ. It is not a wage to be
earned, but a gift to be received from God.
When you ask the Lord Jesus to come into your
heart through faith, He forgives your sins and
you are given an eternal home in heaven.
This is a promise that God has given because of
His great love for you. He wants very much
to welcome you into His family.

*God wants you to know Him,
love Him, and obey Him.*

Grace Is a Gift Because of God's Goodness

Christ gave each one of us
the special gift of grace.
Ephesians 4:7a

By God's loving grace, you are created in the image of God. Your life is an unfinished portrait, but God knows you perfectly and loves you completely just the way you are. You are His masterpiece—His workmanship of grace and love—His work of art. As you grow, He will continue to paint the color of your life in such a way that you will glorify Him. Though your life remains on the canvas, God has seen the finished portrait.

His eternal eyes know exactly where
you need His greatest attention.

God Wants Even the Children to Praise Him

*You have taught children and babies
to sing praises to you.*

Psalm 8:2

When you hear someone singing praises to God,
the very sound and words will resonate with
you. God has placed within your heart a natural
desire to praise Him. Sing of God's love, mercy,
and grace. The more you hear about God's love,
the seeds of wanting to know God will grow and
become the beautiful flower of His blessing.

*When the seed of God's love is planted early,
it will bear much fruit.*

This Is the Way, Walk in Truth

Nothing gives me greater joy than to hear that my children are following the way of truth.

3 John 4

From the moment you are born until you are an adult, the time you spend developing the way of truth will pay dividends of joy and peace within your heart. When you walk in truth and believe in the Word of God, the power of the Holy Spirit will surround you and bring great joy to you. There is no substitute for knowing the truth about your Creator.

You can share God's joy when you walk in truth.

Worry Is Not Part of God's Plan

*Give your worries to the Lord, and
he will take care of you.*

Psalm 55:22

As you grow and learn that you will not get
everything you want, the topic of worry and
frustration will become a reality. Learning to
accept what you cannot have will bring you
security. When you give your worries to
the Lord, He has promised to take care
of you. When you learn this lesson,
the road to finding God becomes easy.

*The Lord is the One true Friend
that will always stand by you.*

God Is the Great Provider

*God can give you more blessings
than you need.*

2 Corinthians 9:8

God has blessed you, and His grace will hold
you up. Every step you take and every word
you speak, God is there encouraging you to be
everything He has planned for you to be.
God wants an abundant life for you, and
His grace will make that possible.

God wants the very best for you.

68

God Has Given You His Blessing

Jesus has the power of God, by which he has given us everything we need to live and to serve God.

2 Peter 1:3

Everything you will ever need to become more like Christ, God has already provided for you. You are like an open book waiting to receive His blessings. You do not need some new experience to help you draw closer to God. You simply have to use what He's already given you. Speak of God's love, and you will be blessed.

Use God's blessings to live and serve Him.

Listening Is a Very Important Lesson

Come to me and listen;
listen to me so you may live.
Isaiah 55:3

Before you can speak one word, you will be
listening to what is being said. Hearing words
of comfort and joy will bless you. When you
share the love of God, you will be blessed.
You have an open invitation to come to God at
any time day or night and enjoy His company.

When you learn to listen, God will speak to you.

Pleasing God Is a
Learned Process

Try to learn what pleases the Lord.

Ephesians 5:10

As you grow, you will naturally learn many
things. What you say and do is important to
who you will become. Your thoughts and words
should bring honor and glory to God. He intends
for His children to become beacons of light to
show the way to spiritual safety for others.

A shining light brings hope.

71

God's Word Is a
Road Map for Life

*I love your commands more
than the purest gold.*

Psalm 119:127

God's Word is a priceless treasure designed
to show you His love and direction for life.
When you read His Word and learn His
commandments, you will build a strong
foundation for your life. As you learn your way
in the world, God's Word can be the compass to
show you what is truly important in life.

You never get lost when you live God's way.

Everyone Needs Wisdom

Learning your words gives wisdom.

Psalm 119:130

One of God's greatest desires is that you
gain wisdom and understanding of His Word.
The Bible says wisdom is "better
than rubies, and all the things one may desire
cannot be compared with her." (Proverbs 8:11
NKJV) When you plant the seed of God's Word
in your heart, it will grow and become fruitful.
There are many distractions in today's culture.
The wisdom that God provides will help
you make the right choices.

Knowledge and understanding come from God.

73

God Never Breaks a Promise

Guide my steps as you promised.
Psalm 119:133

God stands ready and willing to guide your steps
each and every day. Do not hesitate to ask for
His guidance. You need the love, care, and gentle
touch that only God can give. Each step you take
and each word you speak will be blessed when
God is an important part of your life.

*God's promises are like a searchlight that cuts
through the darkness and leads you to safety.*

74

Joy Is One of God's Gifts

Be full of joy in the Lord always.
I will say again, be full of joy.

Philippians 4:4

The joy of the Lord is a gift given to
everyone who walks with God. When you
learn stories from the Bible about God's truth,
you are planting seeds of joy and contentment.
As you grow, there will be certain challenges
and difficulties you will face. Learning to rejoice
at all times in spite of the circumstances will
depend on your relationship with God.

Plant your seeds early, and a
fruitful garden will grow.

Everything Comes from God

*Remember, God is the One who
makes you and us strong in Christ.*

2 Corinthians 1:21

You are God's special gift. He has given His Spirit
to be with you in all that you do. Seek God daily
for His wisdom. As you grow in the Lord and let
go of your own will—He will become the focus
of your life. His love will surround you and fill
you with His presence. His mercy and grace are
like new beginnings every morning.

*God has placed His Spirit in your heart to be
a guarantee for all He has promised.*

76

God Accepts You

*Make every effort to give yourself to God
as the kind of person he will approve.*

2 Timothy 2:15

God calls us to draw near to Him and to His Son,
Jesus Christ. When you open your heart to the
Father, everything you say and do will flow into
place. Live each day with the joy that only
God can give. The Lord is on your side.

Growing closer to God is a choice.

Jesus Christ Is Your Model

You are God's children whom he loves,
so try to be like him.

Ephesians 5:1

As a child of God, you are called to be more
like Him. The thoughts you think and the
words you speak should show the person
you are becoming in your Christian walk.
When you speak kind words, you will encourage
others. Seek God's blessing, and the love of
God will flow through you.

As a child of God, be like your Heavenly Father.

78

God's Word Prepares
You for Life

My child, pay attention to my words;
listen closely to what I say. Don't ever forget
my words; keep them always in mind.

Proverbs 4:20–21

God's desire for you is to learn what He has to
say about the words you speak, the thoughts you
have, and how you treat others. He has a special
plan designed just for you. If you listen to what
He says in His Word, you will be blessed
and God will be pleased.

Change begins in the mind.

God Lives in You

We are the temple of the living God.
2 Corinthians 6:16b

When you let God into your life,
He dwells within you through the Holy Spirit.
It's a relationship unlike any other and promises a
multitude of rewards. You will never regret
a life lived with Christ.

*God has promised to live with you
and walk with you.*

God Keeps His Promises

We can trust God to do what he promised.

Hebrews 10:23b

The one person you can always trust is God. Whatever He has promised, He will do. The Bible is filled with many promises for your life, and all are designed to be a blessing to you. Everything you need can be found in God's promises.

God's promises are true.

81

God Knows Everything About You

You saw my body as it was formed.
All the days planned for me were written
in your book before I was one day old.

Psalm 139:16

God knew everything about you
even before you were born, and He knows
everything about you now. He knows
your weaknesses and strengths, and still
He loves you just the way you are.
He wants to be close to you.

You are a child of God.

Great Is Your God

*My dear children, live in him so that when
Christ comes back, we can be without fear
and not be ashamed in his presence.*

1 John 2:28

God wants you to live in such a way that
every step you take and every word you say
pleases Him and makes you a blessing to others.
When you live in Christ, the way you act
shows God's unconditional love.

God never changes.

83

Learn from the Bible

Children, come and listen to me.
I will teach you to worship the Lord.

Psalm 34:11

As you spend time learning God's Word,
He will show you the life He desires for you.
If you read and hide God's Word in your heart,
it will become a trusted guide and come to
you later when you need it most.

Lessons learned early can last a lifetime.

84

You Are Chosen

God has chosen you from among your friends;
he has set you apart with much joy.

Psalm 45:7b

You are truly God's precious gift.
God has a special plan for your life.
As you walk hand in hand with God,
He will bless you with peace, joy, and
the happiness that only He can give.

God has great plans for you.

85

Show-and-Tell God's Way

Lord, tell me your ways. Show me how to live.
Psalm 25:4

The Lord is waiting to show you how to live,
act, and be more like Him. When you come
to Him in prayer, He will tell you through
His Spirit the things that are pleasing to Him.
The Bible says, "This is the way, walk in it."
(Isaiah 30:21 NKJV) Listen to what God
has to say, and you will be blessed.

God is your guide and teacher.

86

The Holy Spirit Is Your Guide

I will guide you and watch over you.

Psalm 32:8b

Listen to your parents. God uses them to
guide you and help you become the person
He wants you to be. In the same way,
God will also guide you through His Spirit.
You need only to ask, and He will always be
there. When you open your heart to
your heavenly Father, He will shower you
with His love.

He is with you every hour of every day.

Life With the Lord Begins With Hope

*All you who put your hope in the
Lord be strong and brave.*

Psalm 31:24

When you place your hope in the Lord,
you will find that many questions you have
will be answered. God wants you to be strong in
what you believe. When you place your trust in
the Lord, He watches over you wherever you go.

God gives you strength.

Depend on His Word

Hold on to my words with all your heart.
Keep my commands and you will live.

Proverbs 4:4

God's Word has been written just for you.
It is what you do with it that matters most.
You are God's child, and He has given you the
power to live for Him when you apply His Word
to your life. God invites you to be strong in the
Lord and to look to Him every day.

Hold on to His Word with all your heart.

When We Ask for Help, God Answers

I asked the Lord for help, and he answered me.

Psalm 34:4a

When you ask God for help, He is always ready, willing, and able to answer. You are important in God's eyes, and He wants to help you. If you are willing to ask, God has promised to listen.

Depend on the Lord,
and He will watch over you.

God Is the Great Comforter

You, Lord, have helped me and comforted me.

Psalm 86:17b

God has promised to be your Comforter.
He will lift you up. He is there to listen and
comfort you. He is the One that will stick closer
than a brother. Come to God, and He will give
you all the comfort you will ever need.

God is waiting just for you.

91

You Have a Friend in Jesus

A real friend will be more loyal than a brother.
Proverbs 18:24b

You will make many friends and have people you
will be close to in life. God has promised to be
your closest friend. He will be the One who will
always be loyal to you. He is a true friend.

You can always count on God.

You Will Never Be Left Alone

*The Lord your God will be
with you everywhere you go.*
Joshua 1:9b

When you do God's will in God's way
with God's help, no one and nothing can
stand in the way. When you live in the
presence of God and invite Him into every
area of your life, the joy of the Lord will
surround you and you will be blessed.

*God is with you, no matter where you go
or what you do.*

You Can Always Come Directly to God

You are my hiding place.

Psalm 32:7

You can come to God for safety and comfort.
When life presents you with challenges,
God's goodness is waiting for you.
Let each step you take be filled with His
guidance and love. May each day bring you
closer to the One who has given you life.
He has promised to bless you when you
trust Him with all your heart.

Jesus is waiting for you.

94

Nothing Is Impossible for God

God can do anything!
Luke 1:37

Through God, all things are possible.
As you learn more about Him, you will see
things through His eyes. What may seem
impossible to you is not impossible to God.
He desires that you walk closely with Him
and be happy in all that you choose to do.

With God, all things are possible.

God's Plan for You

Follow Me, and I will make you fishers of men.
Matthew 4:19b (NKJV)

God wants you to follow Him and teach others about Him. During His time on earth, Jesus was teaching, preaching, healing, and instructing people so that they might believe and grow to have a relationship with Him. That relationship is still available to you today.

The choice is yours.

96

God Cares for You

Give all your worries to him,
because he cares about you.

1 Peter 5:7

When you are in your mother's arms
and she gently cares for you, you will
feel secure and protected. As you go to school
and interact with others, there may be times of
worry. God wants you to bring everything to
Him. He always has your best interest at heart
and will use all of His power to help you.

You are always under God's protection.

97

Your Heavenly Father Knows Best

Your Father knows the things you need before you ask him.

Matthew 6:8b

Your Heavenly Father loves you and knows everything about you. You were created in His image, and He wants the very best for you. When you say your prayers, ask Him to fill your heart with His love and be your guide. You are important to God, and He wants you to be happy and glorify Him every day.

Talk to God often in prayer.

The Love for Christ
Begins in Your Heart

*I pray that Christ will live in your hearts
by faith and that your life will be strong
in love and be built on love.*

Ephesians 3:17

You are God's child, and He has placed
in your heart a great desire to love Him.
His love surrounds you and fills you each day
so that you may grow stronger in your faith.
Share the wonderful love of God with others.
When you allow His love to be a part of
who you are, His joy will flow over you.

Enjoy a close relationship with God.

99

You Were Born to Be Blessed

The words of a good person give
life, like a fountain of water.
Proverbs 10:11a

God's Word will sustain you throughout
all of your life. He will protect you and give you
everything you need to learn, grow, and be a
blessing to others. God wants to bless you so
your life and words will bless others.

The words of a good person are like pure silver.
Proverbs 10:20

You Are God's Jewel

The Lord says, "As surely as I live,
your children will be like jewels."

Isaiah 49:18b

You have been created as a special jewel
by God. In His eyes, you are more precious
than diamonds and rubies. His desire for you
is to be the person He made you to be.
That is why He has surrounded you with
His love, mercy, and grace. Let each day be
filled with His presence, and include
Him in all that you do.

When you walk with Him,
He will bless you with His favor.

*If you have enjoyed this book
or it has touched your life in some way,
we would love to hear from you.*

*Please send your comments to:
Hallmark Book Feedback
P.O. Box 419034
Mail Drop 215
Kansas City, MO 64141*

*Or e-mail us at:
booknotes@hallmark.com*